Leadership Lessons Ratan of Bharat

Leadership Lessons Ratan of Bharat

Field Marshal S.H.F.J. Manekshaw

Progressive Youth Series

Virender Kapoor

LEADERSHIP LESSONS RATAN OF BHARAT
Virender Kapoor

Published by Qurate Books Pvt. Ltd.

Published in 2023

ISBN: 978-81-96261-88-7

Qurate Books Pvt. Ltd.
Goa 403523, India
www.quratebooks.com
Tel: 1800-210-6527, Email: info@quratebooks.com

The safety, honor, and welfare of your country come first, always and every time.
The honor, welfare, and comfort of the men you command come next.
Your own ease, comfort, and safety come last, always and every time.

—Field Marshall Philip Chetwode

Table of Contents

Author's Note

SEVERAL BOOKS HAVE been written about this legend, one better than the other, one more exhaustive and elaborate than the other. Then should I write another book on this great man? That was the first question that came to my mind. I wanted to write but like every author, I had to be convinced that I need to write something on this subject.

There were a few reasons which were sufficient for me to chug along and write. The first was that the existing books were very detailed, mostly hard bound and hence very huge or thick which were not written for the masses. Secondly, the price of such books is very steep, mostly upwards of Rs. 800/-and individuals don't buy them. Third, which probably was the most compelling one was that today the youth do not have the patience or the inclination of reading a very detailed account of anyone or anything –however important it may be.

I wanted to bring out the maximum in a minimum number of pages and obviously at a much more affordable price. Therefore I was looking at around 80 pages paperback priced below Rs 100/- so that it reaches the masses. Field Marshall Manekshaw hung his boots as a Chief of the Indian Army in 1973. Anyone born after that must know about him, his character, leadership, and his contribution to the nation.

In the progressive youth series this would be a book based on a real-life hero who took a hit of seven bullets, defeated death as a young captain, and rose to become the Chief of the Indian army, and after the victory of 1971, was made a Field Marshall.

Virender Kapoor

It is fatal to enter any war without the will to win it.

—Douglas MacArthur

The Military Cross

THE MILITARY CROSS (MC) is the second-highest level military decoration awarded to British officers and post 1993 to other ranks of the British Armed Forces too, and formerly awarded to officers of other Commonwealth countries.

Awards are announced in The London Gazette, apart from most honorary awards to allied forces in keeping with the usual practice not to gazette awards to foreigners. The Military Cross was designed by Henry Farnham Burke.

Sir Henry Farnham Burke, KCVO, CB, was a long-serving Anglo-Irish officer of arms at the College of Arms in London. Henry Burke was invested as a Commander of the Royal Victorian Order (CVO) by King Edward VII at Buckingham Palace on 11 August 1902, and was later promoted to become Knight Commander (KCVO) of the Order. He was awarded CB in the 1911 Coronation Honors.

The award was created at the end of 1914 within six months of the start of the First World War.

The MC is granted in recognition of:
"An act or acts of exemplary gallantry during active operations against the enemy on land" to all members of the British Armed Forces of any rank. In 1979, the Queen approved a proposal that a

number of awards, including the Military Cross, could be recommended posthumously.

For the Indian Armed forces, the second-highest gallantry award is Maha Vir Chakra (MVC)

1
Destiny

A man does not make his destiny:
he accepts it or denies it.

—Ursula K. Le Guin.

IT WAS MARCH 31, 1971, when I first saw this great man who was taking the salute as the chief guest at the Passing out parade at the Indian Military academy. During tea time, I got a chance to shake hands with this tall and handsome General. His grip was vice-like and the shake hand was not an ordinary shake, I to date remember the power in his right arm. He was fifty-eight years old and we were still in our late teens! We were lucky and destined to meet him in person—even if it was for a few minutes only. He had seen five wars in his four-decade-long active service and India had won a war with Pakistan liberating East Pakistan (now Bangladesh) just a few months ago under his military leadership. It was an honor for all of us.

Sam Manekshaw was born to Parsi parents on 3rd April 1914 at Amritsar. His father was a Doctor, Dr. Hormizd Manekshaw who decided to move from Gujarat to Lahore in 1903 with his wife Hilla, née Mehta. Since he had friends in Lahore it was a well-thought-out decision. But when the train reached Amritsar station his wife who was pregnant was unable to take the further journey and they had to halt at Amritsar. During their stay they found Amritsar to be a nice and agreeable city and decided to settle down there. Hormizd started his practice in Amritsar and became a well-established doctor. The couple had six children and Sam was the fifth one. His father served as a captain in the Second World War in the British army in the medical service as a doctor.

Sam wanted to become a doctor too- a Gynecologist but his father told him that he was too young and he could with great difficulty pay for his two elder brothers studying abroad and therefore will not be able to afford any additional financial burden. Sam did his initial schooling in Amritsar and then in 1929 went to prestigious Sherwood College Nainital. He did well in school and then joined the Hindu Sabha College (now the Hindu College, Amritsar), and in the summer of 1932 wrote his final exams held by the University of Punjab, passing with the third division in science.

The dice rolls on

The Indian Military College Committee was set up in 1931 and recommended the establishment of a military academy in India to train Indians for officer commissions in the army. With an entry age of 18 to 20 years, a three years officers' training course was proposed. A formal notification for the entrance examination to enroll in the Indian Military Academy (IMA) and examinations were scheduled for June or July.

Sam in an act to rebel against his father for not allowing him to become a doctor applied for this exam. He was one of the fifteen cadets to be selected through open competition, Sam Manekshaw was placed sixth In the order of merit in the selected list of candidates. He was selected as part of the first batch of cadets called "The Pioneers" being the first batch.

Does the walker choose the path, or the path the walker?

—Garth Nix.

At the time of Manekshaw's commissioning, it was customary that newly commissioned Indian officers were initially attached to a British regiment before being sent to an Indian unit. He, therefore, joined the 2nd Battalion, Royal Scots. He was later posted to the 4th Battalion, 12th Frontier Force Regiment.

He was fluent in Punjabi (Born and long raised in Amritsar) Hindi, Urdu, English, and his parental language of Gujarati, Manekshaw also qualified as a Higher Standard army interpreter in Pashto.

In the first two years of the conflict during the Second Great War, he saw action in Burma in the 1942 campaign at the Sittang River with the 4th Battalion, 12th Frontier Force Regiment, and was recognized for bravery in battle. This was a bloody and fierce battle.

During the fighting around he led his company in a counter-attack against the invading Imperial Japanese Army; despite suffering heavy casualties the company achieve its objective. After capturing the objective, he who was leading from the front was hit by a burst of light machine-gun fire and was severely wounded in the stomach. Maj. Gen. David Cowan, commander of the 17th Infantry Division, spotted the brave officer clinging to life and, having witnessed his valor in the face of enemy resistance, rushed over to him. Fearing that he would die, the general pinned his own Military Cross ribbon on him saying, "A dead person cannot be awarded a Military Cross", so let me give it to you while you are still alive (that bad was the condition of Sam at that time). This award was made official with the publication of the notification in a supplement to the London Gazette on 21 April 1942,

The citation was spectacular and it was as given below:

Captain Sam Hormusji Framji Jamshedji Manekshaw, 4 Bn. (Sikh), 12th Frontier Force Regiment

This officer was in command of 'A" Company of his battalion when ordered to counter-attack the Pagoda Hill position, the key hill on the left of the Sittang Bridgehead, which had been captured by the enemy. The counterattack was successful despite 30% casualties, and this was largely due to the excellent leadership and bearing of Captain Manekshaw. This officer was wounded after the position had been captured.

Sam Manekshaw was evacuated from the battlefield by Sher Singh, his orderly, who took him to an Australian surgeon. The surgeon initially declined to treat Manekshaw, saying that he was badly wounded and his chances of survival were very low, Sher Singh forced him to treat Manekshaw. By then young captain Manekshaw regained consciousness, and when the surgeon asked what had happened to him, he replied that he was "kicked by a mule". Impressed by Manekshaw's sense of humor, he treated him, removing a total of seven bullets from the lungs, liver, and kidneys. Much of his intestines were also removed. He must have had the constitution of a bull to survive such an injury.

> What counts is not necessarily the size of the dog in the fight—it's the size of the fight in the dog.
>
> —Dwight D. Eisenhower

Sam Manekshaw, after recovering fully, attended the prestigious eighth staff course at Command and Staff College in Quetta between 23 August and 22 In December 1943, on completion of this course, he was posted as the brigade major to a Brigade. After finishing this tenure he joined the 9th Battalion, 12th Frontier Force Regiment, in Gen. Slim's Army.

On the Japanese surrender, Sam Manekshaw was appointed to supervise the disarmament of over 60,000 Japanese prisoners of war (POWs). There was not even a single case of indiscipline or escape attempts from the camp under his command. He did a six-month lecture tour of Australia. On his return from Australia was appointed a Grade 1 General Staff Officer (GSO1) in the Military Operations (MO) Directorate.

After the Partition of India in 1947, Manekshaw's unit, the 4th Battalion, 12th Frontier Force Regiment, became part of the Pakistan Army, so he was reassigned to the 8th Gurkha Rifles. While handling the issues relating to partition in 1947 he demonstrated excellent skills in planning in his capacity as GSO1. At the end of 1947, he was posted as the commanding officer of the 3rd Battalion, 5 Gorkha Rifles. Before he could move on to his new appointment, at end of October 1947, Pakistani forces infiltrated Kashmir, capturing Muzaffarabad. The next day, the ruler of Jammu and Kashmir, Maharaja Hari Singh, appealed for help from India.

Sam Manekshaw carried out an aerial survey of the situation in Kashmir. According to him, the Maharaja signed the Instrument of Accession on the same day, and he flew back to Delhi. Lord Mountbatten and the Prime Minister, Jawaharlal Nehru, were briefed, during which Manekshaw suggested immediate deployments of troops to prevent Kashmir from being captured.

Indian troops were thereby sent to Kashmir on 27 Oct, and Srinagar was occupied just before Pakistani forces reached the city's boundary. In such critical operational circumstances, Manekshaw's posting order as the commanding officer of 3/5 GR was canceled, and he was posted to the MO (Military Operations) Directorate.

Because of the Kashmir dispute and the annexation of Hyderabad, which was also planned by the MO Directorate, Sam Manekshaw never commanded a battalion. This is usually required for further promotions. But God has his ways. Destiny was playing out but never hampered his progress. During his term at the MO Directorate, he was promoted to colonel, then brigadier when he was appointed as the first Indian Director of Military Operations. This appointment was later upgraded to major general and then to lieutenant general, and is now termed Director General Military Operations (DGMO). This is a prestigious appointment and now there was no looking back for Sam.

With the troops once again

Manekshaw already a Brigadier in staff, was appointed the commander of the 167 Infantry Brigade, headquartered at Firozpur, Punjab at the young age of 38 years in 1952.

To command is to serve, nothing more and nothing less.

—Andre Malraux

2

A Man of his Men

Because the crew was convinced that I was "on their team" there were never any issues with negative criticism... You as a mentor have to establish that you are sincerely interested in the problems of the person you are mentoring.

*—Ret. Capt L. David Marquet, US Navy,
and author of Turn the Ship Around!*

A unique motivational style

As mentioned in the last chapter, he could never command a unit, an Infantry battalion because of the circumstance. He had great respect for the Gorkhas whom he never commanded. He could never actually decide which of the two regiments 5 or 8 Gorkhas he liked more, so he carried two lanyards representing both regiments. This was an honor for both the Paltans as they are fondly called.

He was so impressed by Gurkha troops that he would swear by their bravery. He once said which became very famous.

"If a soldier says he is not afraid of death, he is either lying or he is a Gorkha."

There is a lot in a name

This deep admiration was enthusiastically returned by the Gorkhalis — Sam Bahadur remains a popular household name among the community. There's also an interesting tale about the origin of 'Sam Bahadur', the moniker Manekshaw was affectionately known by.

Harka Bahadur Gurung, a Gurkha soldier serving in the Quarter Guard (a ceremonial guard mounted at the entrance of a military unit) was accosted by Manekshaw, who barked: "Mero naam ke ho? (What's my name?)".

Without batting an eyelid, the Gurkha soldier smartly responded, "Sam Bahadur, saab." The military hero loved the quick riposte and the name stuck forever.

After being commissioned, Sam was attached to the 2 Royal Scots. Since his name was a tongue twister for the British officers of the Scottish Regiment, they abridged it to "Mr. Mackintosh"!

> Whether an atom bomb is necessary or not, in this world if you want to be recognized, if you don't want to be kicked about, you have to be powerful both militarily and economically.
>
> —Sam Manekshaw

He could lock horns with politicians.

Today neither the senior Bureaucrats nor the Army generals have the guts to do what he did.

Sam Manekshaw was a man impervious to political pressure. He once surmised,

"I wonder whether those of our political masters who have been put in charge of the defense of the country can distinguish a mortar from a motor; a gun from a howitzer; a guerrilla from a gorilla, although a great many resemble the latter."

How uniquely true this is for India because the western nations including the US had several top leaders who had served their army including President Eisenhower and Winston Churchill.

From fighting off the government's attempt to downsize the army (in what came to be known as Plan 100) to frequent skirmishes with defense minister VK Krishna Menon, Manekshaw's razor-sharp wit almost landed him in trouble on several occasions.

But he was saved by the fact that no one ever doubted that he would uphold the oath he had taken while joining the army. As he said while giving the inaugural Field Marshall KM Cariappa memorial lecture in 1996,

"There is a very thin line between being dismissed and becoming a Field Marshall."

Such a forthright response is perhaps unthinkable today.

An encounter of a different kind in high places.
At a meeting in Delhi Y.B Chavan, the then defense minister, asked Manekshaw his views on which army command Sam considered most important, challenging, and threatening. Eastern Command, said the general, as it had the Chinese in the North, East Pakistan in the South, and on its flank, insurgency rampant in Nagaland and the Mizo Hills; and if all that was not enough to fill the hands of the incumbent, the troubled state of West Bengal certainly would. Chavan thought over the answer for a few moments and then asked if Sam would like to accept the challenge of taking over that command. He accepted immediately.

Handling such a vast responsibility hands-on
Lieutenant General Depinder Singh (retd) in an interview with Rediff says[1],

---

1 https://www.rediff.com/news/2003/apr/03sam.htm

"Eastern Army had to keep one wary eye directed north on the Chinese; another eye had to be kept on erstwhile east Pakistan which lay in its gut, it had to fight insurgency in Nagaland which later spread to the Mizo Hills, and finally it had to watch over the politically volatile states of Assam and West Bengal. It was, therefore, no bed of roses, and the job of lower formations was not facilitated by the army commander's personally coming on the telephone every now and then and 'grilling' staff officers and commanders with endless questions about detail.

I remember an occasion in Shillong where I once asked the senior staff officer why he was looking a bit off-color. He told me he had just finished a telephone conversation with the army commander who had wanted answers to so many questions that, 'I am now in an orbit.'

His mastery of detail was fantastic and, as I was to learn later, he could quote an answer given verbally or in writing months previously to correct someone who was saying something else. A battalion employed in the Mizo Hills, paying perhaps a little more attention to the welfare of its troops and, in the process, a little less than desirable to the operational side received a rude reminder that 'someone up there' was watching, very keenly, every move that was made. A parcel of bangles was delivered to the commanding officer with the compliments of the army commander with a cryptic note: 'If you are avoiding contact with the hostile give these to your men to wear." Needless to say, the next few weeks saw a flurry of activity by this battalion resulting in another, more soothing message: 'send the bangles back.'"

These are the ways of great people.

A man for all seasons

Sam Manekshaw was able to demand courage from his soldiers because his own was never in doubt and he had amply demonstrated it on the battlefield.

Manekshaw commanded great respect worldwide in the military world which was bestowed on him when he visited Nepal after liberating Bangladesh, by King Mahendra, by conferring on him the title and sword of Honorary General of the Royal Nepal Army.

He always fought in his unique way for what was due to his troops and this is something that is withering away in modern armies.

I say, 'Make the best of your destiny'

Once there was a cut in the soldiers' uniform allowance. He decided to take matters into his own hands and invited the members of the Pay Commission to his room. He was impeccably dressed, as always. He walked up and down in his room pensively as if thinking something deeply before uttering anything. After some time, he turned to the members in the room and said "Now gentlemen, you tell me, who would obey my orders if I was dressed in a crumpled dhoti and kurta?" Such were the tales of Sam Manekshaw's ingenuity. Thus, the debate on the uniform allowance came to an end.

Jehan Manekshaw, Sam Bahadur's grandson was much attached and close to him and in an interview he said,

"Whenever I have had the privilege to meet army officers, they shake my hand as soon as they know who I am.

They say thank you and I wonder why they thank me, but I realize they want to honor my grandfather's memory. They are pleased to meet me because they get to reminisce about him.

It is through the eyes of army officers and soldiers that I realize what a figure he was for them.

He represented a value system and stood up for the soldier.

There was something right and good about what he did during his time in the Army. Soldiers have not forgotten that.

Soldiers talk about his leadership, integrity, courage, and professionalism as a soldier. These were the values that Sam wanted the army to have and not be corrupted by external agencies and politics.

When you hear army officers and men talk about that you know they are yearning for the same thing."[2]

For a soldier who became a legend and an icon of India's military leadership, Field Marshall Manekshaw wore his greatness very lightly and Jehan explained how.

"He said that his life was 99% hard work and 1% luck, but for that 1% luck, one had to put 99% hard work.

He had done all the hard work and when the opportunity came, it thrust him into the limelight and made him the person in charge at the most critical time.

He was a professional soldier. He told the politicians of the day that if the war was to be won, they would have to listen to him.

In a lecture on leadership in St Xavier's College, Mumbai, which is on YouTube, he said beware of the yes man.

He was concerned about the culture of sycophancy that was starting to take root in politics and the army.

He was grounded and humble because he recognized that first and foremost, he was just a human being."

"Once you do that then it is very easy to carry your greatness lightly," he said.

Anyone who served him or briefly met him was in awe of this great man.

Nitin Gokhale is Security & Strategic Affairs Editor, NDTV, and visited Defense Services Staff College at Wellington in Nilgiris several times to deliver a lecture to the student officers.

On one such occasion, he was driven by Sam Manekshaw's Driver who had known the Field Marshall for two decades. The name of the driver was Hridayraj but his father nicknamed him Kennedy as he was born the day US President Kennedy had been assassinated and his dad like most in the world thought of John F Kennedy as a good man.

---

2 https://www.rediff.com/news/interview/jehan-manekshaw-the-sam-i-knew/20211216.htm

Gokhale didn't miss this opportunity and learned a lot about Sam Manekshaw firsthand about Manekshaw as an officer and a gentle man.[3]

"What a great man he was," recalled Kennedy.
"Whenever I went to his house with the staff car from the college (Defence Services Staff College) when Sam Manekshaw was the commandant, the first thing he would tell Solai (the Field Marshall's batman), Kennedy ko chai pilao, bread mein jam lagao, butter lagao! Each time, without fail, the Field Marshall would make me eat the bread-butter and drink tea," an emotional Kennedy remembered. "The Field Marshall had cows at home. The household made its own cheese," he added.

"He was a pucca soldier, Sir. He would never eat his breakfast without getting fully dressed. Also, he always used to deliver the last lecture of the day for the staff course."

He was an honest man and lived frugally he remembered when he said...

"Very often Madam (the Field Marshal's wife, Silloo) would drive him to the market in her Maruti 800. He would purchase the essentials from the market himself – vegetables, meat – he loved doing that,"

"You know something Sir, he bought the plot of land in 1960 when he was commandant of the Staff College, but even as a major general, he did not have enough money. He told me once 'Kennedy, I had to take out money from my provident fund to buy this land.'"

"The Field Marshal never said it openly, but Madam and other family members often made it clear that they were never happy with the way the government treated him after retirement. They gave him the baton, 5 stars, and nothing else," Kennedy said. "Not even a dedicated car," an angry Kennedy recalled.

---

3 https://www.rediff.com/news/column/when-kennedy-drove-the-legend-ary-sam-manekshaw/20130304.htm

"You know Sir, President Kalam was the one who gave him more dignity than anyone else. I drove the President to the hospital where the Field Marshall was admitted during his last days," Kennedy recalled.

Kennedy was extremely angry at how the government treated the Field Marshall in death. "No chief came for his burial. Defense Minister A.K. Antony sent his junior minister. Is this the way we treat our heroes Sir?" he asked.

Remembering with his boots on the ground

Lt General AS Kalkat was army commander & former commander Indian Peace Keeping Force (IPKF), Sri Lanka and he recalls the way Sam Manekshaw came to them on the western front during the war with Pakistan in 1971 when he was the Chief and Kalkat a Lt Col.

'I remember an incident in December 1971, he recalls, which underscores the rapport the army chief had with his men and his indomitable valor. Such a long time ago but not long enough for me to forget even an hour of those days. I was then a lieutenant colonel commanding the 5/8 Gorkha Rifles, which belonged to Sam Manekshaw's regiment, the 8 Gorkha Rifles.

Always do everything you ask of those you command.

—General George S. Patton, U.S. Army

We were deployed in the Chhamb sector where the most ferocious fighting of the 1971 Indo-Pakistan war took place. While the operations against the Pakistan army in East Bengal (now Bangladesh) were launched by the Indian Army after Pakistan's atrocities against the Bengalis in East Bengal and everyone's attention was on it, Pakistan launched a pre-emptive attack in the Western Theatre in Chhamb.

By now, it was a full-blown war on both fronts. Pakistan had some initial successes due to the surprise factor and overran the Indian brigade defending Chhamb. By this time, the Indian Army had reacted and deployed the 68 Brigade occupying the East Bank of the River Tawi. While the Tawi was not deep and the infantry could wade through it in most areas, there were only two possible crossings for tanks near the Chhamb Bridge over Tawi and the other about three kilometers south opposite a village called Darh. My battalion was deployed to defend the Chhamb crossing and another battalion was deployed to defend the Darh crossing. I had already demolished the bridge so that Pakistanis could not reach us.

Consequently, the divisional commander ordered me to launch a counter-attack. I launched the counter-attack soon after sundown in the darkness and after very fierce fighting and heavy casualties on both sides we succeeded and drove the Pakistani forces back across the river Tawi. The progress of our action was being monitored by an anxious army headquarters and the chief of the army staff General Manekshaw was informed immediately. He was away at the Eastern Theatre overseeing the operations against East Bengal which led to an eventual surrender.

That night the Pakistanis attacked Darh with tanks and after fierce fighting, they were able to establish a bridge head at Darh by the morning. While the reserve forces of our Brigade were able to prevent the bridge head from going deeper, Pakistan was rapidly building up more forces in the bridge head during the day and it was assessed that during the night they would be able to have sufficient forces to launch a thrust towards Akhnoor about 25 KM east of Chhamb where the bridge over the Jammu Tawi was located. Its loss would have severed the eastern part of Jammu and Kashmir (J&K) from India and enabled Pakistan to attack Jammu from the rear, thus cutting off J & K from India.

The first thing the next morning, Sam Bahadur was with us. He had come personally to compliment the soldiers for their brave actions. He insisted on going right up to the forward positions. The subedar sahib cautioned that going up to the forward positions would draw enemy fire, especially if they had any inkling of who was in the field. Sam nonchalantly waved aside the objection saying: "Don't worry, let them know that I am here. They wouldn't want to tangle with me. In any case, they are bad shots and will probably miss me." Then striding forward he looked back at the subedar sahib and said with a twinkle in his eye. "Now, you be careful, sahib, they might get you instead." With that, off we went to the forward positions. The Pakistani soldiers were still on the ridges above and looking down at us. For whatever reason, no one fired even one shot. Throughout the light-hearted camaraderie of those hours with Sam, the men could see the steel behind those green eyes and it left them with renewed resolve and hope.[4,5]

He respected those who were close to him and always helped them

"I was to see a great deal of Sher Singh (Who saved his life by taking him to the hospital when he was hit by seven bullets) during my tenure in Delhi," says Lt Gen Depinder Singh, author of the book *Soldiering with Dignity* on Sam Manekshaw. He and some other grizzled old veterans of the 4/12 Frontier Force Regiment were frequent visitors to Army House and South Block. The entire staff including all guards and sentries had strict orders that if a man said he was from the 54th Sikhs he was to be led straight to the Chief, whatever the time or whatever the Chief happened to be doing," he adds.[6]

____

4 https://www.hindustantimes.com/analysis/remembering-the-life-and-times-of-sam-manekshaw/story-70BtnQCBlQOh1ja9cRnDJK.html

5 https://english.jagran.com/sports/give-your-best-when-sam-manekshaw-inspired-indian-hockey-team-to-a-golden-finish-in-1980-moscow-olympics-10030121

6 https://www.rediff.com/news/2003/apr/03sam.htm

A man with a golden heart

When Manekshaw turned 90, Jehan and a young filmmaker, Jessica Gupta, convinced him to talk about his life for a documentary film as part of the UNESCO Parzor Project. In the film, Jehan could be seen asking Manekshaw about his greatest achievement in life. "From the ranks of the second lieutenant to Field Marshall, I have never punished a man," replied Manekshaw. "I would sign court-martial proceedings when the verdict was not guilty. But if it said guilty, I would take the file home and look at it and then would say no. They would question my decision, and I would tell them that sitting happily in Delhi they had no idea what those chaps on the ground are going through."

Manekshaw's Pep talk inspired the Indian Hockey team to a Golden finish in the 1980 Moscow Olympics

Indian Men's Hockey team made it to the semi-finals of the Tokyo Olympics by defeating Great Britain 3-1 on a Sunday. Last India had made it to the Top 4 in Olympics, it was in Moscow 1980 games, where amid a mass boycott of Olympics due to Soviet invasion of Afghanistan, India finished on top of the podium to clinch the Gold medal.

Hockey great Vasudevan Baskaran, who captained India's way to the top of the podium in Moscow games, says that Field Marshall Sam Manekshaw's motivation played a key role in pushing Indian Hockey players to pull off their best in Moscow. "The Field Marshall came in person to watch the team train and he spoke to the players. He was the one who made me the captain, and he said it was not because of my seniority, but looking at the future of Indian hockey," Baskaran was quoted as saying by *rediff.com*.

"His confidence-oozing talk remained with me all through the Olympic Games. He had said, 'You look tough and you have a fire in your belly,' he told me. Pass this on to your teammates. They are young and can play with speed. Play well and you will finish on the podium."

Leadership is the art of getting someone else to do something you want done because he wants to do it."

—Dwight D. Eisenhower

3

Leadership Style of Sam Bahadur

Give me a man or a woman with a common sense and decency, and I can make a leader out of him or her.

—Sam Bahadur

LEADERSHIP I ALWAYS argue is an art and not a science. Second, Leaders are born as well as made.

Some of this art you inherit or is gifted by God and some for most they develop. None of us is so unlucky as to have zero leadership traits. Everyone has leadership in some measure for sure: certain traits are strong while some others are not that strong.

Another important thing to understand and accept is that you are a manager for the first few years in your job and after that, your role automatically gets redefined as a leader. In every profession at every level, you are a leader. A CEO, Political leader, School principal, even a class teacher is a leader. Where ever you deal with people leadership comes into play.

In the armed forces as an officer, you have to be a leader from day one. This privilege is a big responsibility too. You are leading men into battle or in treacherous areas. Yet as you progress and put in more years in service, your own leadership style emerges. If you work with good leaders you imbibe some good qualities from them too.

Sam Manekshaw did emerge as a great leader and at every level, he demonstrated great leadership traits. As a young captain in Second World War when he was seriously injured or as Chief of the Army Staff in 1971 when he led India into victory by defeating Pakistan Army and liberating Bangladesh.

If we look at our own nation, Of 1.4 billion strong do we wonder why we are not better or at Par with Germany? Or even Singapore and Hong Kong? We have brains, we have the numbers and we have resources and raw materials. Yet we are not there. I feel it is leadership that matters. Even if you change the principal of a school and college it impacts the performance depending on the leadership qualities of the person on top.

Field Marshall also firmly believed that good leadership makes all the difference.

According to Sam Bahadur, there are six cardinal principles of leadership. *It is good that he didn't list 50 of them. It proves the point that a leader must be precise and brief.*

Here are briefly his six principles in his own words while delivering a lecture a DSSC Defence Services Staff College, Wellington on Leadership and Discipline on 11th November 1998.

The first, the primary, indeed the cardinal attribute of leadership is professional knowledge and professional competence. Now you will agree with me that you cannot be born with professional knowledge and professional competence even if you are a child of a Prime Minister, the son of an industrialist, or the progeny of a Field Marshall. Professional knowledge and professional competence have to be acquired by hard work and by constant study. In this fast-moving technologically developing world, you can never acquire sufficient professional knowledge. You, therefore, need to be at it at every rank.

Ladies and Gentlemen, professional knowledge and professional competence are a sine qua non of leadership. Unless you know what you are talking about, unless you understand your profession, you can never be a leader.

Unless you are professionally competent you can neither lead your people nor can you accomplish your mission.

It is the ability to make up your mind to make a decision and accept full responsibility for that decision. Have you ever wondered why people do not make a decision? The answer is quite simple. It is because they lack professional competence, or they are worried that their decision may be wrong and they will have to carry the can. Ladies and Gentlemen, according to the law of averages, if you take ten decisions, five ought to be right. If you have professional knowledge and professional competence, nine will be right, and the one that might not be correct will probably be put right by a subordinate officer or a colleague. But if you do not take a decision, you are doing something wrong. An act of omission is much worse than an act of commission. An act of commission can be put right. An act of omission cannot. At levels of responsibility, you are paid to take tough yet appropriate decisions.

The impact and repercussions of your decisions become more and more palpable as you get more responsibility. If you are good and competent you will falter less and less.

When I was the Army Chief, I would go along to a formation, ask the fellow what have you done about this and I normally got an answer, "Sir, I have been thinking... I have not yet made up my mind," and I coined a Manekshawism. If the girls will excuse my language, it was 'if you must be a bloody fool – be one quickly'. So remember that you are the ones who are going to be the future senior staff officers, the future commanders. Make a decision and having made it, accept full responsibility for it. Do not pass it on to a colleague or subordinate.

The next for leadership is absolute Honesty, fairness, and justice – we are dealing with people. Those of us who have had the good fortune of commanding hundreds and thousands of men know this.

No man likes to be punished, and yet a man will accept punishment stoically if he knows that the punishment meted out to him will be identical to the punishment meted out to another person who has some Godfather somewhere. This is very, very important. No man likes to be superseded, and yet men will accept supersession if they know that they are being superseded, under the rules, by somebody who is better than they are but not just somebody who happens to be related to the Commandant of the staff college.

We in India have tremendous pressures- pressures from the Government, pressures from superior officers, pressures from families, pressures from wives, uncles, aunts, nieces, nephews, and girl-friends, and we lack the courage to withstand those pressures. That takes me to the next attribute of Leadership- Moral and Physical Courage.

I do not know which of these is more important. When I am talking to young officers and young soldiers, I should place emphasis on physical courage. But since I am talking to this gathering, I will lay emphasis on Moral Courage. What is moral courage? Moral courage is the ability to distinguish right from wrong and having done so, say so when asked, irrespective of what your superiors might think or what your colleagues or your subordinates might want. A 'yes man' is a dangerous man.

He may rise very high, he might even become the Managing Director of a company. He may do anything but he can never make a leader because he will be used by his superiors, disliked by his colleagues, and despised by his subordinates. So shallow – the 'yes man'.

Say what you mean and mean what you say.

—Gen George Patton

Ladies and Gentlemen, there is a very thin line between becoming a Field Marshall and being dismissed.

Let me share an encounter with PM Indira Gandhi where her senior cabinet ministers were present.

A very angry Prime Minister read out messages from Chief Ministers of West Bengal, Assam, and Tripura. All of them saying that hundreds of thousands of refugees had poured into their states and they did not know what to do. So the Prime Minister turned round to me and said: "I want you to do something".

I said, "What do you want me to do?"

She said, "I want you to enter East Pakistan".

I said, "Do you know that that means War?"

She said, "I do not mind if it is war"

I, in my usual stupid way, said, "Prime Minister, have you read the Bible?" And the Foreign Minister, Sardar Swaran Singh (a Punjabi Sikh), in his Punjabi accent said, "What has Bible got to do with this?", and I said, "the first book, the first chapter, the first paragraph, the first sentence, God said, 'let there be light'' and there was light. You turn this round and say 'let there be war' and there will be war. What do you think? Are you ready for a war? Let me tell you –"it's 28th April, the Himalayan passes are opening now, and if the Chinese gave us an ultimatum, I will have to fight on two fronts".

Again Sardar Swaran Singh turned round and in his Punjabi English said, "Will China give an ultimatum?"

I said, "You are the Foreign Minister. You tell me".

Then I turned to the Prime Minister and said, "Prime Minister, last year you wanted elections in West Bengal and you did not want the communists to win, so you asked me to deploy my soldiers in penny pockets in every village, in every little township in West Bengal. I have two divisions thus deployed in sections and platoons without their heavy weapons. It will take me at least a month to get them back to their units and their formations. Further, I have a division in the Assam area, another division in Andhra Pradesh, and the Armored

Division in the Jhansi-Babina area. It will take me at least a month to get them back and put them in their correct positions. I will require every road, every railway train, every truck, and every wagon to move them. We are harvesting in the Punjab, and we are harvesting in Haryana; we are also harvesting in Uttar Pradesh. And you will not be able to move your harvest.

I turned to the Agriculture Minister, Mr. Fakhruddin Ali Ahmed, "If there is a famine in the country afterwards, it will be you to blame, not me." Then I said, "My Armored Division has only got thirteen tanks which are functioning."

The Finance Minister, Mr. Chavan, a friend of mine, said, "Sam, why only thirteen?"

"Because you are the Finance Minister. I have been asking for money for the last year and a half, and you keep saying there is no money. That is why."

Then I turned to the Prime Minister and said, "Prime Minister, it is the end of April. By the time I am ready to operate, the monsoon will have broken in that East Pakistan area. When it rains, it does not just rain, it pours. Rivers become like oceans. If you stand on one bank, you cannot see the other and the whole countryside is flooded. My movement will be confined to roads, the Air Force will not be able to support me, and, if you wish me to enter East Pakistan, I guarantee you a hundred percent defeat."

"You are the Government", I said turning to the Prime Minister, "Now will you give me your orders?"

Ladies and Gentlemen, I have seldom seen a woman so angry, and I am including my wife in that. She was red in the face and I said, "Let us see what happens". She turned round and said, "The cabinet will meet at four o'clock in the evening".

Everyone walked out. I being the junior most man was the last to leave. As I was leaving, she said, "Chief, please will you stay behind?" I looked at her. I said, "Prime Minister, before you open your mouth, would you like me to send in my resignation on grounds of health, mental or physical?"

"No, sit down, Sam. Was everything you told me the truth?"

"Yes, it is my job to tell you the truth. It is my job to fight and win, not to lose."

She smiled at me and said, "All right, Sam. You know what I want. When will you be ready?"

"I cannot tell you now, Prime Minister", I said, but let me guarantee you this if you leave me alone, allow me to plan, make my arrangements, and fix a date, I guarantee you a hundred percent victory".

So, Ladies and Gentlemen, as I told you, there is a very thin line between becoming a Field Marshall and being dismissed. Just an example of moral courage. Now, those of you who remembered what happened in 1962, when the Chinese occupied the Thang-la ridge and Mr. Nehru, the Prime Minister, sent for the Army Chief, in the month of December and said, "I want you to throw the Chinese out". That Army Chief did not have the Moral courage to stand up to him and say, "I am not ready, my troops are not acclimatized, I haven't the ammunition, or indeed anything". But he accepted the Prime Minister's instructions, with the result that the Army was beaten and the country humiliated.

Remember, moral courage. You, the future senior staff officers and commanders will be faced with many problems. People will want all sorts of things. You have got to have the moral courage to stand up and tell them the facts. Again, as I told you before, a 'yes man' is a despicable man.

> What is moral courage? It is the ability to distinguish right from wrong and having so distinguished it, being prepared to say so, irrespective of the views held by your superiors or subordinates and of consequences of yourself.
>
> —Sam Bahadur

This takes me to the next attribute: Physical courage. Fear, like hunger and sex, is a natural phenomenon. Any man who says he is not frightened is a liar or a Gorkha. It is one thing to be frightened. It is quite another to show fear. If you once show fear in front of your men, you will never be able to command. It is when your teeth are chattering, your knees are knocking and you are about to make your own geography; that is when the true leader comes out!

I am not a brave man. If I am frightened, I am frightened of wild animals, I am frightened of ghosts and spirits, and so on. If my wife tells me a ghost story after dinner, I cannot sleep in my room, and I have to go to her room. I have often wondered why she tells me these ghost stories periodically.

On physical courage as a leader
In World War II, my battalion, which is now in Pakistan, was fighting the Japanese. We had a great many casualties. I was commanding Charlie Company, which was a Sikh Company. The Frontier Force Regiment in those days had Pathan companies. I was commanding the Sikh Company, young Major Manekshaw. As we were having too many casualties, we had pulled back to reorganize, re-group, make up our casualties and promotions.

The Commanding Officer had a promotion conference. He turned to me and said, "Sam, we have to make lots of promotions. In your Sikh company, you have had a lot of casualties. Surat Singh is a senior man. Should we promote him to the rank of Naik?" Now, Surat Singh was the biggest Badmaash in my company. He had been promoted twice or three times and each time he had to be marched up in front of the Colonel for his stripes to be taken off. So I said, "No use, Sir, promoting Surat Singh."

You promote him today and the day after tomorrow, I will have to march him in front of you to take his stripes off." So, Surat Singh was passed over. The promotion conference was over, I had lunch in the Mess and I came back to my company lines. Now, those of you who have served with Sikhs will know that they are a very cheerful lot always laughing, joking, and doing something. When I arrived at my company lines that day, it was quite different, everybody was quiet.

When my second-in-command, Subedar Balwant Singh, met me I asked him, "What has happened, Subedar Sahib?" He said, "Sahib, something terrible has happened. Surat Singh felt slighted and has told everybody that he is going to shoot you today."

Surat Singh was a light machine gunner and was armed with a pistol. His pistol had been taken away, and Surat Singh has been put under close arrest. I said, "All right, Sahib. Put up a table, a soap box, march Surat Singh in front of me". So he was marched up. The charge was read out: 'threatening to shoot his Commanding officer whilst on active service in the theatre of war'. That carries the death penalty. The witnesses gave their evidence.

I asked for Surat Singh's pistol which was handed to me. I loaded it, rose from my soap box, walked up to Surat Singh, handed the pistol to him then turned round and told him, "You said you will shoot me". I spoke to him in Punjabi naturally. I told him, "Have you got the guts to shoot me? Here, shoot me". He looked at me stupidly and said, "Nahin, Sahib, galtee ho gayaa". I gave him a tight slap and said, "Go out, case dismissed."

I walked around, chatted to the people, went to the Mess in the evening to have a drink, and have my dinner, but when I came back again Sardar Balwant Singh said, "Nahin Sahib, you have made a great mistake. Surat Singh will shoot you tonight".

I said, "Bulao Surat Singh ko".

He came along. I said, "Surat Singh, aj rat ko mere tambu par tu pehra dega, or kal subah 6 bajay, mere liye aik mug chai aur aik mug shaving water lana". Then I walked into my little tent.

Ladies and Gentlemen, I did not sleep the whole night. The next morning, at six o'clock, Surat Singh brought me a mug of tea and a mug of shaving water, thereafter, throughout the war, Surat Singh followed me like a puppy. If I had shown fear in front of my men, I should never have been able to command.

I was frightened, terribly frightened, but I dared not show fear in front of them. Those of you, who are going to command soldiers, remember that. You must never show fear. So much for physical courage, but, please believe me, I am still a very frightened man. I am not a brave man.

> He who speaks without modesty will find it difficult to make his words good.

> —Confucius

On Loyalty

The next attribute of leadership is loyalty. Ladies and Gentlemen, you all expect loyalty. Do we give loyalty? Do we give loyalty to our subordinates, to our colleagues? Loyalty is a three-way thing. You expect loyalty, you must, therefore, give loyalty to your colleagues and your subordinates. Men and women in large numbers can be very difficult, they can cause many problems and a leader must deal with them immediately and firmly. Do not allow any nonsense, but remember that men and women have many problems. They get easily despondent, they have problems of debt, they have problems of infidelity-wives have run away or somebody has an affair with somebody. They get easily crestfallen, and a leader must have the gift of the gab with a sense of humor to shake them out of their despondence. Our leaders, unfortunately, our "so-called" leaders, definitely have the gift of the gab, but they have no sense of humor. So, remember that.

> Imagination was given to man to compensate him for what he is not; a sense of humor to console him for what he is.

> —Francis Bacon

On Discipline

What this country needs is discipline besides good leadership. We are the most ill-disciplined people in the world. You see what is happening- you go down the road, and you see people relieving themselves by the roadside. You go into town, and people are walking up and down the highway, while vehicles are discharging all sorts of muck. Every time you pick up a newspaper, you read of a scam or you read of some other silly thing. As we are the most ill-disciplined people in the world, we must do something about discipline.

What is discipline? Please, when I talk of discipline, do not think of military discipline. That is quite different. Discipline can be defined as conduct and behavior for living decently with one another in society. Who lays down the code of conduct for that? Not the Prime Minister, not the Cabinet, nor superior officers.

It is enshrined in our holy books; it is in the Bible, the Torah, and the Vedas. It has come down to us from time immemorial, from father to son, from mother to child.

Nowhere is it laid down, except in the Armed Forces, that lack of punctuality is conduct prejudicial to discipline and decent living.

I will again tell you a little story about that. Some years ago, my wife and I were invited to a convocation at a university. I was asked to be there at four o'clock. I got into the staff car with my wife, having chased her from about eleven o'clock in the morning. Don't forget, darling, you have got to be on time. Get properly dressed; you have to leave at such and such time.

We were received by the Vice-Chancellor and his Lady. We were taken into the convocation hall, and the Vice-Chancellor asked me to get on the platform, asking my wife to do so, too. She gracefully declined and said she much rather sit down below as she seldom had an opportunity of looking up to her husband. Anyway, on the platform, the Vice-Chancellor sang my praises. As usual, there were 2000 boys and girls who had come for the convocation. There were deans of university and professors.

Then he asked me to go to the lectern and address the gathering. I rose to do so and he said, Field Marshall, a fortnight ago we invited a VIP from Delhi for the same function. He was allowed to stand on the same lectern for exactly twenty seconds. I wish you luck. "I said to myself, had the Vice-Chancellor mentioned this in his letter of invitation, I wonder if I should have accepted."

Anyway, I reached the lectern, and I addressed the gathering for my allotted time of forty minutes. I was heard in pin-drop silence, and at the end of my talk, was given a terrific ovation. The Vice-Chancellor and his lady, the Dean, the professors and lecturers, the boys and girls, and even my own wife, standing up and giving me an ovation.

We walked into the gardens to have refreshments. I started a conversation with a young girl. I said, "My dear, why were you so kind to me, I not being an orator nor having the looks of Amitabh Bachhan, when only the other day you treated a VIP from Delhi so shamefully". She had no inhibitions and said

"Oh, that a dreadful man! We asked him to come at four o'clock. He came much later and that too accompanied by a boy and a girl, probably his grandchildren. He was received by the Vice-Chancellor and his lady and taken to the platform. He was garlanded by the Student Union President, and he demanded garlands for those brats too. So, the Union President diverged with the garland that was meant for the Vice-Chancellor and gave it to the brats.

Then the Vice-Chancellor started singing the worthy's praises. Whilst he was doing so, this man hitched up his dhoti, exposing his dirty thighs, and scratched away. Then the Vice-Chancellor said, "This man has done so much for the country, he has even been to jail". And I nearly shouted out, 'He should be there now'. Anyway, when the Vice-Chancellor asked him to come to the lectern and address the convocation, he got up, walked to the lectern, and addressed us thus, 'Boys and girls, I am a very busy man. I have not had time to prepare my speech but, I will now read out the speech my secretary has written'. We did not let him stand there. Without exception, the whole lot of us stood and booed him off the stage.

Now, you see, Ladies and Gentleman, what I mean by discipline. Had this man as his position warranted come on time at four o'clock, fully prepared and properly turned out, can you imagine the good it would have done to these 2000 young girls and boys?

Close encounters of Manekshaw kind - Get the bull by the horns
Field Marshall was straightforward and was not a yes man ever. Maybe that was a reason why the politicians didn't like him. He goes on to explain this himself and I quote,

"Mr. Krishna Menon, the Defence Minister, disliked me intensely. General Kaul, who was Chief of General Staff at the time, and the budding man for the next higher appointment, disliked me intensely. So, I was sent to Staff College in disgrace – a sedentary job. There were charges against me – I will enumerate some of them – all engineered by Mr. Krishna Menon.

I do not know if you remember that in 1961 or 1960, General Thimayya was the Army Chief. He had fallen out with Mr. Krishna Menon and had sent him his resignation. The Prime Minister, Mr. Nehru, persuaded General Thimayya to withdraw his resignation. The members of Parliament also disliked Mr. Krishna Menon, and they went hammer and tongs for the Prime Minister in Parliament.

The Prime Minister made the following statement, "I cannot understand why General Thimayya is saying that the Defence Ministry interferes with the working of the Army. Take the case of General Manekshaw. The Selection Board has approved his promotion to Lieutenant General, over the heads of 23 other officers. The Government has accepted that."

I was the Commandant of the Staff College. I had been approved for promotion to Lieutenant General. Instead of making me the Lieutenant General, Mr. Krishna Menon levied charges against me. There were ten charges, I will enumerate only one or two of them – that I am more loyal to the Queen of England than to the President of India, that I am more British than Indian. That I have been alleged to have said that I will have no instructor in the Staff College whose wife looks like an ayah. These were the kind of charges against me.

For eighteen months my promotion was held back. An enquiry was made. Three Lieutenant Generals, including an Army Commander, sat at the enquiry. I was exonerated on every charge. The file went up to the Prime Minister who sent it up to the Cabinet Secretary, who wrote on the file, 'if anything happens to General Manekshaw, this case will go down as the *Dreyfus case.*' So the file came back to the Prime Minister. He wrote on it, "Orders may now issue", meaning I will now become a Lieutenant General.

Instead of that, I received a letter from the Adjutant General saying that the Defence Minister, Mr. Krishna Menon, has sent his severe displeasure to General Manekshaw, to be recorded. I had it in the office where the Commandant now sits. I sent that letter back to the Adjutant General saying what Mr. Krishna Menon could do with his displeasure, *very vulgarly stated. It is still in my dossier!*

Then the Chinese came to my help. Krishna Menon was sacked, Kaul was sacked and Nehru sent for me. He said, "General, I have a vigorous enemy. I find out that you are a vigorous General. Will you go and take over? "I said, "I have been waiting eighteen months for this opportunity," and I went and took over.

"I was at DSSC for eighteen months, persecuted, inquisitions against me but we survive."

I had to turn the ship around and I had to go hammer and tongs.

The first order I issued was

"Gentlemen, I have arrived and there will be no withdrawal without written orders and these orders shall never be issued."

I feel that if you are competent and take a stand it works- but one has to be prepared to go down too. Which is not easy to do.

Leaders give credit to others

When Dr. APJ Abdul Kalam had come to Symbiosis International University, I was present, he addressed the staff, faculty, and students. He had told the gathering about earning respect as a leader which he had learnt from his boss prof Satish Dhawan at ISRO where

Kalam was the Project manager directly responsible for the launch of the satellite in 1979.

Kalam overruled his team who had some reservations about the success and ordered it to go ahead. The launch failed; instead of going into space, the satellite plunged into the Bay of Bengal. As a team leader, Kalam was very uncomfortable with facing the press. He was saved from embarrassment by the chairman of ISRO, Satish Dhawan, who went himself before the television cameras to say that despite this failure he reposed complete faith in the abilities of his team and was confident that their next attempt would succeed.

Not only that, when his team tried once more to launch a satellite into space and succeeded; Dhawan congratulated the team, and asked Kalam to address the press conference. He said, "It is your victory, you should be in front of the camera."

A great lesson to learn is that "When the failure occurred, the leader owned it up. When the success came, he gave the credit to his team."

Great leaders do this and Field Marshall Manekshaw was great too- especially in this regard.

The incidence below says it all.

He was commanding the war from Delhi and hence was in the capital when the war was won.

He could have easily flown to Dacca to take the surrender from Pakistani General AAK Niazi, but he chose not to. He had his General Officer Commanding-in-Chief of Eastern Command Lieutenant General Jagjit Singh Aurora, Chief of Staff Eastern Command Lt Gen J F R Jacob, General Officer Commanding 4 Corps Lt General Sagat Singh among others to accept the instrument of surrender.

He even told General Aurora to take his wife along. He felt this was a moment she would remember.

He was not one to come and pose for the photograph.

He remembered his commanders very fondly not only for what they did in the war but also as people. He would crack jokes and play pranks.

He was a great people person. If you were in front of him, he took an active interest in you.

Beyond the 'sir' and the 'salute', there was a man who actually cared about his officers and men and that's what made him a great leader.

This demonstrates a good character of a tall leader, which most fail to demonstrate.

> It is amazing what you can accomplish if you do not care who gets the credit.
>
> —Harry S Truman, 33rd President of the United States, and former Colonel in the U.S. Army

Another incidence of being a great man of character goes like this

On his return from a higher command course in England, he was appointed the General Officer Commanding (GOC) 26th Infantry Division. While he commanded the division, Gen. K. S. Thimayya was the Chief of the Army Staff (COAS), and Krishna Menon was the defense minister. During a visit to Manekshaw's division, Menon asked him what he thought of Thimayya. Manekshaw replied that it was not appropriate for him to think of his chief in that way, as he considered it improper to evaluate his superior, and told Menon not to ask anybody again. This annoyed Menon, and he told Manekshaw that if he wanted to, he could sack Thimayya, to which Manekshaw replied, "You can get rid of him. But then I will get another."

> A true leader has the confidence to stand alone, the courage to make tough decisions, and the compassion to listen to the needs of others. He does not set out to be a leader, but becomes one by the equality of his actions and the integrity of his intent.
>
> — Douglas MacArthur, General of the U.S. Army

4
Style and Substance

*Style is a reflection of your attitude
and your personality.*

—Shawn Ashmore

SAM MANEKSHAW WAS an officer and a gentleman. Born in April, he shared the sun sign Aries with greats like Otto von Bismarck, Thomas Jefferson the Founding Fathers of the USA, and the principal draftsman of the Declaration of Independence as well as General Collin Powell Joint Chiefs of Staff chairman and later US secretary of state.

All of them were great successful men who contributed to their nation's might in one way or the other. Like a typical Aries Manekshaw was great to be with. Was strong, brave, and took up challenges. Refused to be manipulated was plain-speak and truthful to the tee. Energetic, sure-footed, quick to make decisions, and a kind personality.

He and his wife Silloo were great hosts and fond of calling people home for a party.

Their refrigerator was always packed to the brim with exotic delicacies, from Russian caviar to canned fish, many of which would remain inside the fridge long after they had crossed their expiry dates. They had a big deep freeze. He loved the famous Parsi dish called Dhansak. Sam loved cooking and his barbeque parties were the talk of the town.

Manekshaw's had elaborate barbecue cookware those days and these would come in handy while hosting dinners. Those who have experienced his gracious hospitality recall him as being an excellent host. He would never let waiters serve drinks to his guests. He would do it himself. During barbecue evenings at home, he would be turning the skewers himself and would expect his guests, too, to do the same. The food was never pre-cooked and all the fresh salads would be from his garden.

They always had homegrown fruits and vegetables, milk, and eggs that they would happily give to the entire neighborhood. Manekshaw in a way was fond of gardening and enjoyed it. He would wake up at six, put on his shorts and tee-shirt, and work in the garden for two hours every day.

He loved good cars

Sam had a Charismatic persona. He loved to live life king size and in style.

He had a silver color Austin Sheer line car which was his favorite.[7]

The Austin Sheer line is a large luxury car produced by Austin in the United Kingdom from 1947 until 1954.

The Sheer line was designed by Austin during the Second World War, but volume production did not begin until 1947 because of the commitment to war production. It was a luxurious car in the style of the contemporary Rolls-Royce or Bentley but at a much lower price, around two-thirds that of the equivalent Rolls-Royce but still the price of five or six small Austin's. There were about 8,000 built. It had a 4000 cc powerful engine and sheer luxury on wheels.

He also was fond of another car, Sunbeam Rapier.

---

7 https://www.magzter.com/stories/News/THE-WEEK/SHADES-OF-SAM

In matters of style, swim with the current; in matters of principle, stand like a rock.

—Thomas Jefferson

Would go out of the way to help

In the year 1969, a celebrity wedding took place in Calcutta. Sam Manekshaw was the Army commander of Eastern Command Headquartered at Fort William Calcutta. It was the wedding of actor Sharmila Tagore a Hindu and Mansoor Ali Khan Pataudi, Indian cricket captain and Nawab of Pataudi. A huge protesting mob gathered outside the venue of the wedding reception party. The high-profile interfaith marriage had led to communal polarization in Bengal and it became a major problem to ensure safe passage for the couple.

When Manekshaw learned this, he sent his own car to rescue them. As tension continued to mount, a silver color Austin Sheer line car arrived to pick up the newlyweds. His car was as famous as Manekshaw and the crowd didn't have the guts to stop it! It perhaps saved the couple as they made their way out of the club. In his eagerness to help, Manekshaw prevented what could have been a massive tragedy that day.[8]

God makes such people too

When Manekshaw rose to higher ranks, Silloo never demanded special privileges. Both of them remained grounded and humble. For instance, although they were entitled to a house call when unwell, they would go to the armed forces clinic, stand in the queue, collect their tokens and see the doctor.

In later years, he settled down for a retired life at distant Coonoor from the hustle-bustle of power-centric Lutyen's Delhi where he was promised a permanent bungalow by the then Government. He had

---

8 https://www.theweek.in/theweek/cover/2021/12/04/sam-manekshaw-through-the-eyes-of-his-family-and-friends.html

built his own house in Wellington, a beautiful Military station, calm quiet and lush green, a heaven on earth. He named his abode Stavka. A really creative thought. As many may not know this word.

The Stavka was the high command of the armed forces in the Russian Empire and the Soviet Union. In Imperial Russia, Stavka refers to the administrative staff, and the General Headquarters in the late 19th-century Imperial Russian armed forces and subsequently in the Soviet Union.

He remained active there till the ripe age of ninety and was invariably a star attraction in many functions as he charmed everyone with his magnetic personality.

He maintained his humor and wit notwithstanding his advancing age. He kept a respectful distance from officers of the Indian Armed Forces as a principle. He never interfered in their functioning although his advice was always much sought after. He was aware that he had allowed nobody to interfere in his functioning while he was in service and therefore made it a point not to interfere when he was out of it.

He inspired men and women who came in contact with him in his life after retirement. He along with his wife carried out charitable work for local tribes in Connor. His personal physician Dr. Shinde had mentioned to Lt Gen (Dr.) Prasad that late Field Marshall used to wait for his turn in his clinic whenever he visited for a health check. No tantrums or pushing his way through- a thorough gentleman. When he visited Dr. Prasad at Army Hospital (R&R) where he was posted there as a Chest Physician, he was witness to his respect for doctors. He says and I quote:

"Despite prior appointments, like any other abiding patient, he used to wait for his turn in my busy OPD before entering my chamber and then lie down on the examination couch after removing his shoes with readiness to submit his body for thorough physical examination by loosening his clothes and turning his face the other way with few deep breaths. After the examination, he was eagerly keen to know my opinion and then ask me invariably whether I had consulted his personal doctor however junior he may be. He used to take my opinion seriously and the opinion given by another doctor should be respected and can't be brushed aside. His family members were respectful and lived up to his values.

He ensured that all who visited were really taken care of. Whenever I called on him to enquire about his health he used to ensure that his son-in-law treated me well with choicest drinks and food. He was concerned about me till the very end. Though he was frail and weak and breathing heavily, the moment I entered his ward a few days before his death, he opened his eyes and looked at my face to recognize me instantly even in those dying moments, and enquired, "Col Prasad are you, all right? Did you have your food?"

He never used Army facilities for his family and sternly warned his family members against any misuse. His son-in-law Dhun Daruwala who cared for him all through in later years politely declined to use Army medical facilities for his own use despite he had suffered from a serious ailment. His children never used his staff car. His beloved daughters both Mrs. Sherry Batliwala and Mrs. Maza Dharuwala kept him in good humor and ensured that he was really cared for. His grandson Jehan Daruwala who adored him from his heart like his other brother Raul even changed his surname to Jehan Manekshaw.

His concern for his Gurkha family who looked after him in Coonoor was phenomenal. He really cared for them- enhanced their salary, gave decent education to their children, and ensured them a good living conditions in the quarters adjacent to his Bungalow. During his time, it was compulsory for all staff course officers belonging to the Gurkha battalion to have a meal with him at his bungalow even at his ripe age.

> I believe that a simple and unassuming manner of life is best for everyone, best both for the body and the mind.
>
> —Albert Einstein

Loved his people: A story worth telling

After retirement, Sam Manekshaw settled in Coonoor. Everyone knew he had two daughters. He was dependent on MH (Military Hospital) at Wellington about eight kilometers away.

One night the duty medical officer- a young captain got a call from Sam Manekshaw that his daughter was not well and he would bring her to the hospital. He also told the young doctor not to inform his Commanding officer. Sam was against making any fuss and disliked preferential treatment.

The doctor saw Manekshaw's sunbeam car from which the Field Marshall got down and was seen helping a young woman to get down. Sule Bahadur his batman was also there. Captain ensured everything was ready.

As Sam's daughter was being examined by the young captain Manekshaw asked in a concerned tone, "Is she too bad?"

The doctor told him that she would be fine soon. The doc asked the young lady some general questions in English. She looked back with blank eyes and stammered, "Khui, kooni, hui, hui."

The young captain got alarmed and suspected damage to her brain and the changed circumstances demanded a more thorough examination. He told the nurse to make her comfortable on the examination bed behind the screen. In the meanwhile, Sam and his Gorkha batman left the room.

He gave the young lady an injection and was contemplating calling in the full arsenal of specialists. The batman came in and sat on the patient's bed. He started petting the lady on her head and then even held her hand.

What are you doing? Leave her hand. Get away from her, you chap," the Captain snapped at him. Sule Bahadur looked at him as if deeply hurt and said. "Sahib, am I not allowed to hold my ailing wife's hand in your MI room?"

The dense fog in his mind parted. So, she was the batman's wife. How shallow were his powers of observation! The Field Marshall treated his staff's families like his own.[9]

He who stops being better stops being good.

—Oliver Cromwell.

____

9 https://www.tribuneindia.com/news/comment/when-manekshaw-drove-to-hospital-334903

5
Humor was his Trademark

*A person without a sense of humor is like a wagon
without springs. It's jolted by every pebble on the road.*

—Henry Ward Beecher

SAM BAHADUR WAS not only Bahadur but had a great sense of humor. He could be sardonically sarcastic as well. With a perfect idea of timing and the event, he could fine-tune his remarks remarkably. He could crack a joke with a naughty glint in his eyes almost at will.

So much so he could crack a joke with the surgeon when riddled with seven bullets in his body and almost facing death! You got to have humor in your blood to do so and I am sure he had plenty of it.

He could do with his juniors, seniors, ladies, and even in a serious cabinet meeting.

There is nothing more important for a man than to have a good sense of humor. It not only makes you a pleasant personality but also, at times, helps you handle tricky or sticky situations. A sense of humor gives you that additional edge over your competitors—and costs you nothing.

A small humorous incident or a nice little pun or joke at an appropriate time can be a great value addition to your otherwise daily mundane life. Timing, context, and audience are very important to add humor to our lives, without annoying others.

Why is humor being referred to as a "sense of humor"? Because you need to have a sense of timing and understanding of what kind of humor is appropriate for what occasions. Therefore, humor should be used with a bit of caution, so that you don't hurt someone unintentionally. As a rule of thumb, you should never laugh at the expense of someone else. This is viewed as being rude or sarcastic. It is an important aspect that you be careful not to use humor in a context that makes you look silly—what we call "putting your foot in your mouth." Humor also reflects a person's level of intelligence and level of understanding human emotions and relationships. I am sure that to come up with jokes, understand jokes, and enjoy them, you require a good enough IQ. Haven't you often seen some duffers who can't understand a joke?

Mr. N. Vittal, IAS, the Former central vigilance commissioner (CVC) is known for his wit and humor and is popularly called "Witty Vittal." Since I know him personally, I've had opportunities to discuss many things with him. He would always come up with something extremely witty during his discussions, addresses students, or even to the media.

He used to deliver talks in colleges, and my students used to look forward to his sessions on a variety of subjects because he used to make his interactions with students very lively and witty. I had met the late advocate Ram Jethmalani on several occasions, and what made him such a good speaker and a likable person was his wit and humor. What pages of text cannot say, one humorous remark may say it all.

The legendary Akbar-Birbal short stories and anecdotes are full of humor. Yet each one of them conveys a thought process, a solution to a problem, or a strong message. This is the power of humor in our lives. Please remember that as a leader you could use humor to keep everybody's morale high or keep them in high spirits.

A good laugh makes any interview, or any conversation, so much better.

—Barbara Walters

Humor can come in very handy in making presentations. Today, the attention span of individuals is very short. How do you keep them as active participants throughout your presentation? Humor is the answer.

No wonder today a large portion of the content on social media is humor- people love it and look forward to it. Tik Tok and Whatsapp is making the world laugh like crazy.

A few years back, at the US-India Strategic Dialogue, while addressing the audience, President Obama said, "Oh! Now we have a new item on the menu—'Hillary Platter,'" referring to a dish that was specially prepared by the Indian chef. Even in high-level diplomacy, humor, if used appropriately, can be very effective.

Leaders or bosses who are witty are always liked by their people. They instill a lot of brightness in a day's work. Please remember, nobody likes to work with someone who is always serious and never laughs.

A sense of humor is God's gift and a great one too. People with a sense of humor can find humor in anything and light a spark in everybody's life, including their own. You don't have to be a stand-up comedian as a teammate but should have enough of a sense of humor to get along. Everybody may not be gifted with humor, but one can make efforts—and I assure you, one can succeed.

The highest sense of humor is to be able to laugh at yourself. This is done by those who are very self-assured and don't bother about the world. It's a tall order, but some people do have it in them.

Field Marshall Manekshaw did have the audacity to laugh at himself.

I remember a function organized by a professional forum to felicitate people who were bestowed Padma awards. Obviously, they were all movers and shakers in their own domains.

One of these celebrities could not reach on time and the function had to start, with the chair at the head table earmarked for him left unoccupied.

This high profile gentleman was none other than Cyrus S. Poonawalla the chairman and managing director of the Cyrus Poonawalla Group, which includes the **Serum Institute of India,** an Indian biotech company, which is the largest vaccine manufacturer in the world. In 2022, he is ranked number four on Forbes India rich list with a net worth of $24.3 billion.

After fifteen minutes or so, Cyrus Poonawalla entered and the president of the forum, who was on the mike, looked at his watch and said, "Oh my God! Cyrus has, at last, arrived," obviously taking a dig at him. Cyrus immediately responded wittily, "Thanks, I am glad for a change you have started on time!" Everybody in the audience laughed.

This, I call, 'turning the tables humorously'.

The brigadier and his wife, Zenobia, who have published the book Field Marshall Sam Manekshaw: The Man and His Times, spoke to THE WEEK over a Zoom call from the US. "She would not be bothered about protocol," he said. Panthaki shared an anecdote from a Republic Day function when they were at the Rashtrapati Bhavan. Around 25 VVIPs were invited for tea. "While we were walking to the VVIP enclosure, the Field Marshall was ahead and Mrs. Manekshaw was a few steps behind him. A security officer stopped her, saying that her name was not on the guest list. The Field Marshall heard that and told the officer, 'Yeh toh meri biwi hai. Aapko maloom nahin hai ki iska gussa bahut kharab hai? Isko mat roko aur aane do mere saath (She is my wife. Don't you know how bad her temper is? Don't stop her. Let her come with me).'" It got sorted.

This is how Sam Manekshaw got around a serious subject with the pay commission.

The outbreak of the Second World War saw the 4/12 Frontier Force Regiment in action in Burma with the famed 17 Infantry Division. Sam was separated from his family for over three years and this separation was the cause of a celebrated example he was later to give while answering questions put to him in his capacity as Chief of the Army Staff by the Pay Commission. The question, which triggered off the reply was, why should the army continue to get separation allowance? This, to clarify, is a token sum every officer and enlisted man gets when his unit moves to a non-family station thus necessitating separation. I say 'token' because the name is a misnomer; whereas it is meant to cover the expenditure incurred in running two establishments, the amount paid is, in fact, a pittance. For example, an officer used to get just seventy rupees a month and the men an even smaller amount.

The answer to explain the need was "After my marriage, I went off to war and didn't see my wife for three long years, and when I returned I found I had a brand-new daughter, and the only reason I am sure the child is mine is because she looks just like me." Needless to say, the Pay Commission broke up in laughter but went away convinced. The separation allowance continues.

Almost always finishing his own work in an hour, he would often spend the rest of his time floating from one office to another, dropping in on harried juniors and eagerly helping them with their tasks. In fact, his colorful language and irreverent jokes were known to set off tidal waves of mirth through the army headquarters.

Another one goes like this

A story few people know is that, at the time of the Partition, Manekshaw and Agha Muhammad Yahya Khan (the third President of Pakistan) used to work together on the staff of Field Marshall Sir Claude Auchinleck. Their job was to help out with the additional administrative duties that Partition brought along with it.

After Partition, when the two military officers parted ways, Yahya offered to buy Manekshaw's red James motorcycle. (The James Cycle Co Ltd., Birmingham, England, was one of many British cycle and motorcycle makers based in the English Midlands, particularly Birmingham. Most of their light motorcycles, often with the characteristic maroon finish. James was a prolific bicycle and motorcycle manufacturer from 1897 to 1966)

He promised to send over a princely sum of Rs. 1000 from Pakistan. Manekshaw agreed and Yahya took the bike with him.

However, as it turns out, Yahya never got around to sending the payment. After India's victory in the 1971 and the Instrument of Surrender being signed on December 16, Manekshaw was heard saying,

"Yahya never paid me the Rs. 1000 for my motorbike, but now he has paid with half his country," said Sam Manekshaw.[10] [11]

---

10 *https://timesofindia.indiatimes.com/readersblog/come-on-india/the-man-inside-sam-manekshaw-34397/*

11 *https://www.thebetterindia.com/136527/sam-manekshaw-field-Marshall-india/*

6

A Family Man

"A man with good reputation among friends, not necessarily have the same reputation within family."

— *Amit Kalantri, Wealth of Words*

Field Marshall had both.
Manekshaw often said Silloo his wife was both his ardent supporter and his harshest critic. She was the wind beneath his wings, and she was also the one who kept him grounded. I feel this is a very important role of a wife and also credit goes to the man too, for acknowledging this.

A flamboyant young captain Manekshaw married Silloo Bode in 1939. He "swept her off her feet" at a dinner party in Lahore. Silloo was visiting her sister in Lahore whose husband was a doctor in the British Indian army "Sam was quite aware that he was extremely charming and good looking. But mother would put him straight," says his elder daughter Sherry Batliwala. "Silloo would remind him that he came from a middle-class family in Amritsar. 'They would venerate you today, but tomorrow when you are no longer the Field Marshall or the director of a company, you would be a nobody' she would warn him. I think that kept him a little focused and grounded too.[12]

Manekshaw's younger daughter, Maja Daruwala, said there was no fight for control and no concept of gender-defined roles to adhere to in his family. "Although mom was at home, she would not be expected to cook," said Maja, a lawyer, and human rights advocate.

She spoke about the time in 1957 when Manekshaw was sent to the Imperial Defence College, London, to attend a course. "He would do all the cooking for the family without ever once making it look like a chore," she said. "At the time, I was a fussy eater. Yet, he would cook for us all. He was superb at making chhole bhature, kheema pao, makki di roti, sarson ka saag, and bhuna chana soup. He never imposed his military discipline on us. During holidays, we would sleep till 10 a.m. and he would leave us alone, although he loved to have breakfast with us. Even when it came to his hobbies such as fishing and photography—he had all the state-of-the-art equipment—he never forced them upon us. We were, however, always turned into reluctant scapegoats for his experiments!

There was a lot of teasing going around in the house, mostly aimed at Manekshaw by the three women, especially when it came to aesthetics. Silloo, an alumna of Mumbai's Sir J.J. School of Art, was an exceptionally talented artist and painter. Her paintings adorned the walls of every house the family stayed in. Their own home, Stavka, was a majestic bungalow with terrace gardens nestled in picturesque Coonoor in Tamil Nadu's Nilgiris ranges. They had purchased the plot way back in 1960 for a princely sum of Rs 1500. She conceptualized and designed the bungalow from start to finish. It served as their retirement haven.

"Oh for him, madam's word was final. The Field Marshall was a loving father and grandfather. One of his grandsons looked exactly

---

12 www.theweek.in/theweek/cover/2021/12/04/sam-manekshaw-through-the-eyes-of-his-family-and-friends.html

like him. Long nose, tall and fair. I never saw him scold anyone. And he was always kind to people like us. When madam passed away, he was a broken man. We knew he wouldn't last long without his biggest strength," Kennedy said his driver clearly choking.[13]

His grandson Jehan Manekshaw remembers him with respect awe and love and fondly says,

"I would often spend the summers with him. I lived with my grandparents and was enrolled in a school in Coonoor in Nilgiri Hills for a year when my parents were posted someplace else.

He was a brilliant, hands-on grandparent. He would dress me up in the morning. He set a routine -- meals at fixed times, playtime in the garden for 2-3 hours, spending time constructively at home, etc. He made sure I was a well-looked-after kid."

He further adds, "Since we were based in Delhi and Bombay, we would get a chance to meet him when he came to attend board meetings after retiring from the army. He used to serve on the boards of several companies and would be put up at the Oberoi Hotel. I would take an overnight bag, hang out at his hotel room and have club sandwiches, milkshakes, watch TV and skip my homework!"

"He was frequently in our lives. We would see him every two months or so. I was very close to him.

His advice to us was 'Family is most important in life. Love your family and choose any career, but do your best to be the best.'"

Brigadier Behram Panthaki (retd), who authored a book on Sam Manekshaw and who had served as ADC (aide-de-camp) to Manekshaw from 1965 to 1971, said Silloo his wife was quite unassuming despite being the wife of a senior officer.

Zenobia, Brigadier's wife reminisced about a lazy relaxed afternoon at Manekshaw's bungalow Stavka. A potluck, which was common at the bungalow, was in progress, and Manekshaw suddenly

---

13 https://www.rediff.com/news/interview/jehan-manekshaw-the-sam-i-knew/20211216.htm

exclaimed with great excitement, saying that the chaand raat (the crescent moon, which is considered to be highly auspicious by the Zoroastrian community) fell on his birthday that year. He paused for a moment and said, 'But this is as per the British almanac, so will it be chaand raat in India also?' Pat came Silloo's reply. 'Who made him Field Marshall? Iski akal dekho (Look at his intelligence).'" He would take such jokes sportingly.

Manekshaw was Sam to everyone, even to his two daughters and his three grandchildren—Sherry's daughter, Brandy, and Maja's sons, Jehan and Raoul-Sam. To his grandchildren, Manekshaw was the man who never doled out career advice, who would repeat his jokes 500 times over, who expected them to know the name of each rare rose breed in his garden, who was a hoarder with cabinets full of unopened old wines and vodka, and who would drive down to Coimbatore airport in his Sunbeam Rapier to receive them whenever they came visiting. Jehan now runs a drama school in Mumbai, while Raoul-Sam works for a tech firm in the US. Brandy lives in Goa and works in the hospitality sector.

"The strength of a man is in his character. A strong man is a great man of wisdom who understands, his top priority is to his family."

— Ellen J. Barrier,
The Price We Must Pay for Our Father's Sins

7

He could Motivate till his Last Day

*"Our dead are never dead to us, until
we have forgotten them."*

—George Eliot

FOR COLONEL (NOW Lt Gen) BNBM Prasad from the Army medical corps the reason for joining the Army as a doctor was Field Marshall Manekshaw, and as luck would have it, he was there with him till his dying day.

Prasad was doing his MBBS at Mysore Medical College and the country defeated Pakistan in 1971 under the military leadership of Sam Manekshaw. He like many others got motivated to join the army instead of looking for a lucrative job in civilian life.

Though he joined the army in 1977, he had the honor of listening to his address to the cadets at the Passing Out Parade at IMA Dehradun.

He would eventually be appointed personal physician to the Field Marshall but could personally meet his hero only in 2003 when the Field Marshall visited Research and Referral (R&R) hospital in Delhi for his respiratory ailment. Prasad now a pulmonary specialist, was in awe of the man who despite his illness demanded no favors and walked slowly in the hospital corridors as people looked at him in awe with bated breath.

Lt Gen Prasad recounts how his illness never became a deterrent to his humor. He once told him

"My father told me if you keep smoking and drinking you will soon die. Doc had I listened to him I would have died a long back"

Prasad recounts that almost a year later while in Bombay (now Mumbai) Field Marshall got exposed to a chill because of his air-conditioned hotel room and was rushed to RR hospital Delhi once again and Prasad was to treat him. Again what he recollects is amazing "Sam Manekshaw politely declined to sit in the wheelchair and walked to the radiology room himself". He was very sick and was to be hospitalized which too was not his cup of tea. Prasad took special permission to treat him at the residence of his daughter in Delhi.

Doctor Prasad also remembers Sam once telling him 'Doc why can't you have scotch in my name? I am sorry I will not be able to give you company and you know why". This was a man different from all others.

Prasad last met him at Wellington hospital when his condition suddenly deteriorated on 22 June while he was called in to treat him. Prasad recalls: "It was sad to see a pale hero gasping for breath, very frail, and with my long experience of dealing with such cases I knew the old man at 94 was very sick and nothing much a doctor could do but pray."

His daughters both flew in as I had told their husbands that he may not last more than 24 hours. But the gritty soldier held on till his entire family was with him. He timed his death to his will as he did with military operations.

As his daughters came in he spoke to them for the last time. Another brief miracle had yet to happen. As his daughters spoke and the moment the name of his late wife Silloo was uttered there was a sudden increase in the oxygen level which was being constantly monitored.

He perhaps had the premonition of death. He told an attending doctor a few days back that he had a skin rash on his arm and the day he dies the rash would vanish.

He passed away in the early hours of June 27 2008 while his daughters held his hand.

The rash had vanished too![14]

A week after he passed away, Col Prasad had a surprise visitor.

Sam Manekshaw's Grandson- Jehan came to meet doctor Prasad with a gift from the Field Marshall, a bottle of scotch with a special note

'Col Prasad, FM sent his apologies that he could not drink this with you.'

"What a grand old man," the doc thought looking at the bottle.

"Death, they say, acquits us of all obligations."

–Michel Eyquem de Montaigne

"A Parsi man destined to be born in Lahore was born in Amritsar, wanting to become a doctor joins the Army and is almost killed in action in Burma, hit by seven bullets, meets his life partner in Lahore and leads the nation into military victory against Pakistan (Lahore now in Pakistan) creating a history of creating another nation (Bangladesh) leaves no choice for the Government for his stellar performance

---

14 https://timesofindia.indiatimes.com/india/the-legacy-of-sam-bahadur-manekshaw-lives-on/articleshow/33175580.cm

but to make him a Field Marshall - first in the nation, settles down in a quiet place in the hills of Nilgiris."

"Yeh jeevan hai... Yehi hai, yehi hai is Jeevan ka rang roop... Yeh Jeevan hai..."

—Anand Bakshi

8

Ratan of Bharat

Only Great men meet the great.
Dr. APJ Abdul Kalam the President of India paid a surprise visit to look up ailing Sam Bahadur at wellington hospital in February 2007. He made it a point to tell the doctors 'Do take good care of him, he is the son of India'. He shook hands with Sam Manekshaw and spent fifteen minutes at his bedside[15].

A lone junior minister attended this great man's funeral.
On the day of the funeral of the son of the soil, there was a deafening vacuum of political will and character. Military top brass too displayed a shameful response as none of the three service chiefs were present.

One can understand that Indira Gandhi wanted to hog all the limelight for the 1971 victory with Pakistan and was miffed with Sam Manekshaw so he was not even paid his monitory benefits on time. What is the point of giving you a cheque when you are on your deathbed?

But such bitter hatred by congress and its stooges against an officer holding the highest rank in the army cannot be condoned.

____

15 https://timesofindia.indiatimes.com/india/lone-minister-represents-govt-at-manekshaws-funeral/articleshow/3173797.c

Prime Minister Manmohan Singh and President Pratibha Patil didn't have the courtesy or decency of reaching out to this grand old man! It is a shameful act at a national level. It can't be an omission but a deliberate attempt to disregard a great national hero.

Manekshaw was on the dot when he had said in an address to DSSC officers on leadership something like this:

"An act of omission is much worse than an act of commission. An act of commission can be put right. An act of omission cannot."

One can understand the compulsions of a PM who had little freedom to take action best known to the whole nation. But even the president, supposed to be the supreme commander of the armed forces was tied up to her chair by some invisible forces?

Even Defense Minister Antony skipped and sent his junior minister of State for Defense M.M. Pallam Raju to represent it at the ceremony.

What a national letdown. They didn't disgrace the grand old man but in this act disgraced themselves.

Leader of Opposition LK Advani telephoned Prime Minister Manmohan Singh on Saturday and sought to know why the national flag was not flown at half-mast in the memory of the Field Marshall, who was widely regarded as the architect of India's victory over Pakistan in the 1971 war. Advani said the PM told him that the matter fell under the purview of the Defense Ministry. "The government would not have had to face this embarrassment had the Field Marshall's rank figured in the Warrant of Precedence," an official said[16].

Army chief General Deepak Kapoor was touring Russia, but what about Airforce and Naval Chiefs? What were they worried about having reached their highest attainable ranks? Again shameful.

---

16 https://www.hindustantimes.com/delhi/missing-field-Marshall-rank-led-to-funeral-goof-up/story-Avnn2NWKaalqqX4SP3gJml.html

Was it not a shame on our own fraternity? I was imagining that had Sam Bahadur been the serving chief and there was someone else the Field Marshall who had finished his innings Manekshaw would have surely gone for his funeral.

'The current bunch of Congress ministers, Man Mohan Singh, Antony, PC, Arjun Singh, Mani Shanker Aiyer are a spineless lot. When Sanjay Gandhi was killed, remember the speed with which he was given a funeral, befitting a Head of state, even as VV Giri's death, at the same time, was overlooked. Looks as if only the Nehru Gandhi family is important, military heroes are meant to be forgotten.'

Above is a post by an Indian citizen in agony in response to the Times of India report.[17]

How did Sanjay Gandhi, a nobody, was in the warrant of precedence may I ask?

In contrast

One would hold the present government in the *highest esteem* if you look at the way tributes were paid to CDS Gen Bipin Rawat.

Prime Minister Narendra Modi and the country's top military brass on Thursday paid homage to India's first Chief of Defence Staff Gen Bipin Rawat, his wife Madhulika, Brig LS Lidder, and 10 more defence personnel at the Palam air base after their bodies were brought to Delhi in a military aircraft. Defence Minister Rajnath Singh, NSA Ajit Doval, Army Chief MM Naravane, Navy Chief Admiral R Hari Kumar, Air Chief Marshal AVR Chaudhari, Defence Secretary Ajay Kumar were among those who paid homage to the deceased at a somber ceremony.

This is a different political class and leadership class apart.

No wonder the world looks up to Narendra Modi as a leader of the times.

---

17 https://timesofindia.indiatimes.com/india/manekshaw-funeral-antonys-face-saving-exercise/articleshow_comments/3177765.cms?from=mdr

Can you be this vindictive politically?

A cheque for back wages of over Rs. 1.16 crore was handed over to the ailing Field Marshall in 2007.

Marshall S.H.F.J. Manekshaw, got it a day after the government decided to pay all surviving Marshalls of the Armed Forces a salary equivalent to that of Service Chiefs. Thank God there was no further delay as if it mattered.

While Manekshaw was appointed Field Marshall in 1973. Dues cleared almost 35 years late. And (Indira Gandhi) the government expected him to attack Pakistan ASAP in 1971 pronto, and win the war too!!

The cheque was handed over to Manekshaw, on April 18, 2007, by Defense Secretary Shekhar Dutt, at the Military Hospital at Wellington in Tamil Nadu, where the 93-year-old Field Marshall was admitted some months ago.[18]

He would sure rest in peace

When he died the entire population of Nilgiris lined up in every available space to pay their last respect to a father figure whom they loved from the depth of their heart.

At his memorial service held at Parsi Anju man in Delhi, a few days after his death, many who gathered there and once his close associates were unanimous on one thing- Field Marshall was an embodiment of magnetic charm, razor-sharp intellect, and humanity to the point of divinity.

---

18 https://zeenews.india.com/news/nation/manekshaw-gets-cheque-of-rs-116-crore-for-back-wages_366540.html

9
An informal chat with Kennedy

*"Always enter like a kitten and leave like a lion.
But NEVER enter like a lion and leave like a kitten.
Always be humble."*

—Carlson Gracie.

I HAPPENED TO be in Wellington, Ooty, in April 2022 and did not want to miss the opportunity of meeting Kennedy who knew Field Marshal for a long period. I was not sure how I would be able to contact him and whether I would be able to contact him. I just had his name!

But everyone knew Kennedy in Wellington Gymkhana Club where I had gone for a short holiday. Within minutes of my asking about him, I got his mobile number. I spoke to him and fixed up a time for him to meet me in my cottage the same evening.

As decided, he was with me sharp at 6 PM. As I was having my tea I offered him some biscuits and tea which he politely declined as he had just come from home after a cup of tea.

I asked him 'Since when did he know the field Marshal?' He told me that he knew the family since 1977 when he was just 13 years old.

'We have a nursery near Sims Park called *Lema Rose,* and we used to supply madam Manekshaw flowers, especially roses.'

'I joined Defense Services Staff College as a driver in 1986 and was assigned duties with the VIP fleet, as a lot many important people visit DSSC the entire year.'

'DSSC looked after his transportation needs and I was his driver whenever he visited Coimbatore for any meeting or had to catch a flight. I drove him up and down on an average three to four times a month, almost 100 kilometers one way. So I had the privilege of being with him on a long three-hour drive each side, which was a rich learning experience besides knowing him as a great person,' he added. Havaldar Suliye was also his Sahayak and a driver.

'Sir he was a very simple man and very frank too. He once told me that he was in love with Wellington and wanted to settle down there only. Though Prime Minister Indira Gandhi had told him that government would give him a nice house wherever he wished, including central Delhi he settled in wellington only in his own home. He told me that he had bought a 4-acre piece of land in 1959/60 for Rs. 1500 and had to take a loan from the provident fund as his salary as a Major General was only Rs. 430 every month.' The two-storied bungalow was built by KN Patel of Connor in 1967/68. The entire panoramic view of DSSC was visible from his balcony.

'He lived a very simple life and never bothered to throw his weight as the only Field Marshal. He had a Fiat Premier Padmini and bought a Maruti 800 in 1984 which he and his wife would drive themselves. He had his prized possession, a Sunbeam 1959 that was kept in an immaculate condition and is still parked in his garage in his Bungalow'.

He was in the Military hospital for 18 months before his demise. President Abdul Kalam visited him in 2007 and asked him if he was getting his pension. 'He had never told anyone about this and sir how could he tell this to any serving officer as he was the Field Marshal and all were junior to him. Abdul Kalam another great man noted this and within a month the Defence secretary came personally to give him his full pension with arrears. Why couldn't they do it on their own?' complains Kennedy.

Field Marshal had narrated to him that when he visited Prime Minister Indira Gandhi in her office, she always got up from her chair and when he asked her why she got up as she was the PM and he was only the COAS, she said, 'You are a Tiger!'

Kennedy adds 'He was such a humble person that at times he ventured into driving his car through the hilly terrain to Coimbatore all by himself. Sir, one day around 9 am I was driving my scooter and FM was coming from the opposite side in his Maruti 800. I stopped in the middle of the road and he waved and said "Kennedy, I am going to Coimbatore, do you want to come?" Sir, he asked me to park my scooter in Sims Park and drove along till that circle and only then asked me to come and drive! He used to sit in the co-driver's seat next to me in his private car. He was a Field Marshal'

Homi Sethna was a person who was also settled in Wellington and was very close to the Manekshaw family. I spoke very briefly to him over the phone and he was happy to learn that I was writing a short book on the FM. His elder daughter Sherry Batliwala was holidaying in their bungalow and I did speak to her on the phone regarding the book.

Kennedy says that they are a Royal family and very polite and respectful to everyone. Both the daughters were thoroughbred and called him 'father' and not dad or papa.

One would have noticed that children of people in authority or celebrities are many times snobbish and sometimes even rude to people like drivers or waiters who service them but his children were very we mannered and polished.

Kennedy recalls that on his 90th birthday they made a huge cake that occupied the entire twelve-seater dining table! FM ensured that a big chunk of cake with two bottles of wine was sent to his home.

They loved animals and had dogs at home.

Mrs. Manekshaw did charitable service for the needy. Manekshaw clinic was established in upper Connor where several doctors used to come and give free medical examinations and services at her request. The government of Tamil Nadu did help them with the upkeep of the clinic.

The Field Marshal helped his staff to educate their children too.

Kennedy is a very soft-spoken person and a thorough gentleman. I think good values rub off you when you work with great people. Both his sons are engineers and doing well in life and Kennedy is proud of them and happy with their achievements.

He is retiring in another year but as of now doesn't have any post-retirement plans.